How We Used to Live

Memories of
HOLIDAYS AND HAVING FUN

By Ruth Owen

Published in 2025 by **Ruby Tuesday Books Ltd.**

Copyright © 2025 **Ruby Tuesday Books Ltd.**

All rights reserved. No part of this publication may be reproduced in whole or in part, stored in any retrieval system, or transmitted in any form or by any means, electronic, mechanical, photocopying, recording, or otherwise, without written permission from the publisher.

Editor: Mark J. Sachner
Design & Production: Emma Randall

Photo credits:
Alamy: Cover & 1 (Trinity Mirror/Mirrorpix), 6 (Hi-Story), 8 (Dave Bagnall Collection), 9T (thislife pictures), 11BL (Prisma by Dukas), 13 (Trinity Mirror/Mirrorpix), 15C (Trinity Mirror/Mirrorpix), 16C (Smith Archive), 17R (Allan Cash Picture Library), 18L (KGPA Ltd), 19T (PA Images), 22 (Classic Picture Library), 23T (Smith Archive); Public Domain: 7; Ruby Tuesday Books: 9BL, 21B, 23BR; Shutterstock: Cover (Osieck/Dja65/Violetta Derkach/Olaf Speier/Nikolay 007), 3TL (Katy's Photos), 3BL (Smileus), 3TR (Nattika), 3BR (Sorin Popa), 4L (Mark Seymour), 4TR (Becky Stares), 4B (Picture Partners), 5L (PaintDoor), 5R (Dja65), 10L (ML Robinson), 10R (Sorin Popa), 11T (Stefano Odorizzi), 11BR (IndustryAndTravel), 12 (Olaf Speier), 14L (Richard Semik), 14R (Katy's Photos), 15T (Photofriend), 16B (inxti), 17L (sutlafk), 18R (Smileus), 19B (Peter Zijlstra), 20R (David Pimborough/Deborah Lee Rossiter/Mattpix/Tiger Images), 23BL (Karkas); Superstock: 5B (ClassicStock), 20L (Culver Pictures), 21 (Devaney Collection).

British Library Cataloguing in Publication Data (CIP) is available for this title.

ISBN: 978-1-78856-424-3

Printed in Poland by L&C Printing

www.rubytuesdaybooks.com

CONTENTS

Looking into the Past 4

Respectable Swimming 6

Fashion for the Beach 8

Steam-Powered Travel 10

A Seaside Fish Supper.......................12

A Working Holiday..............................14

A Hop-Picking Summer.....................16

A Day at the Zoo..................................18

Saturday Morning Pictures...............20

Saturday Night Dancing.................... 22

Glossary, Index, Answers 24

LOOKING INTO THE PAST

In this book, we are going to look at some **historical** photographs and objects from the **past**.

They show how people in Britain had fun and enjoyed holidays in the late 1800s and early 1900s.

We will also hear the real-life **memories** of people who lived during the times in the photos.

Together, photos, objects and memories can help us to learn how we used to live.

1

2

3

Look at the objects on these pages. How do you think they were used for fun?

(The answers are inside the book or on page 24.)

What Is a Century?

We measure history in periods called **centuries**. A century lasts for 100 years. Today, we are in the 21st Century.

1801 to 1900	**1901 to 2000**	**2001 to 2100**
19th Century	20th Century	21st Century

4

5

Many of the photos in this book are from a time that we call "living history". It's a time that people who are still alive today can remember.

What do you think is happening in this photo?

(The answer is on page 24.)

RESPECTABLE SWIMMING

People have always enjoyed a swim in the sea. However, in the 1800s and early 1900s, it was not **respectable** for adults to be seen in a swimming costume.

To change into their swimwear, people hired small, caravan-like **bathing** machines.

As a swimmer got changed inside their bathing machine, a horse pulled it out into the water.

BOGNOR: WEST BEACH FROM PIER.

Bathing machine

The swimmer emerged from a door facing the sea and climbed down steps into the waves.

They could splash and swim privately, without strangers on the beach seeing them!

Men and women did not swim together. In some places, there were even laws that said how far apart men and women should be in the sea.

Bathing machine

Swimming costume

FASHION FOR THE BEACH

Today we head for the seaside in casual clothes such as shorts, T-shirts and Dryrobes.

In the past, people often wore their smartest outfit for a day on the sand.

Many working people only owned some work clothes and one set of clothes for "best".

Therefore, a best dress or even a suit and tie were worn to the beach.

A family on the beach in 1920

Today, swimsuits are made from tight-fitting, stretchy fabrics such as nylon and lycra.

In the early 1900s, these fabrics were not available. So many people knitted their own swimsuits – from wool!

People could buy **knitting patterns** for the latest swimwear styles. They also copied designs they saw in fashion magazines.

1930s woollen swimsuits

A packet containing a 1940s knitting pattern

Evelyn (Born 1943)

"Each summer mum knitted us new swimsuits. They fitted perfectly until you went into the sea. The wool soaked up the water. Then the wet swimsuits got heavier and heavier and became so baggy, they stretched down to our knees!"

STEAM-POWERED TRAVEL

In the first half of the 1900s, most people travelled by steam train when they went on holiday or for a day trip to the seaside.

At a station, families waited to hear the puff, puff of the approaching train.

They climbed onboard the train's carriages, carrying picnics, suitcases and buckets and spades.

Passengers sat in small compartments that seated about 10 people.

Suitcases from the 1940s

Sooty smoke

Carriage

Engine

Vending machine

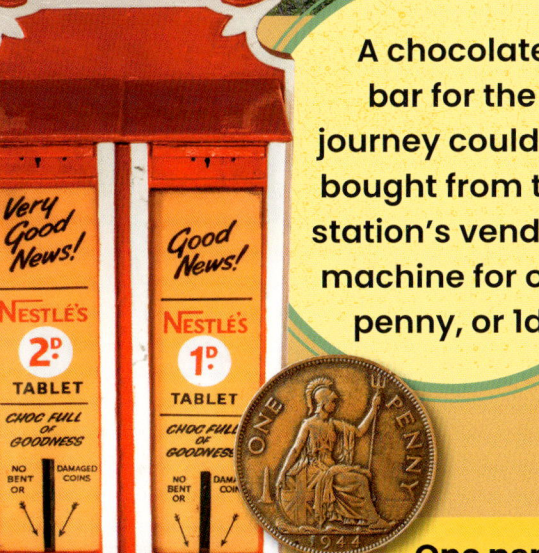

One penny

Rupert (Born 1939)

" Me and my brothers took turns to lean out of the windows. As the train went around a bend, we could see the engine. Sometimes its smoke blew back into our faces. The black, sooty, coal dust in the smoke made our faces filthy. And one day a burning spark from the engine got caught in my brother's hair! "

A chocolate bar for the journey could be bought from the station's vending machine for one penny, or 1d.

A SEASIDE FISH SUPPER

No one knows for sure where or when people first ate fried potatoes or battered fish.

But in Britain, the delicious combination came together as fish and chips in the 1800s.

Just as we do today, people in the past loved to eat this meal – especially at the seaside.

In the mid 1900s, however, there was one big difference from today. Fish and chips often came wrapped in a used newspaper!

Fish and chips in newspaper

John (Born 1940)

" When we went on holiday to Blackpool, we always had fish and chips for tea on the seafront. There were no plastic take-away boxes in those days. Your food was laid straight onto some newspaper. Sometimes you could even spot a little writing or part of an inky picture on your chips! "

Fish and chips for tea in 1954

In the early 1940s, during World War II, there was a paper shortage. So some fish and chip shops began to use newspapers for wrapping food.

Betty (Born 1942)

"Dad bought and read a newspaper every day. We cut up some of them to use as toilet paper. The others were saved. Once there was a big stack in the garden shed, we took them to the fish and chip shop. They used them for wrapping the fish suppers. I guess we were recycling. But we didn't realise it then."

A WORKING HOLIDAY

In the first half of the 1900s, many families from London enjoyed a working holiday.

Travelling by train, they left the smoky, dirty city to pick hops in the green fields of Kent.

Hop field

Hops are the flowers of hop plants. They are used to make beer.

The hop pickers stayed on farms, sleeping in hoppers' huts made of tin or wood. There was no furniture in the huts, except for wooden beds and mattresses stuffed with straw.

Hops

To make their huts more homely, hop-picking families brought bedding, rugs and furniture with them. Some people even brought left-over wallpaper to decorate the walls!

A family arriving in Kent to go hop picking

Barry (Born 1943)

"Sometimes the hop farmer sent an open-backed truck to collect us. Me, my mum, my aunties, my cousins and my nan all rode in the back. We stayed in Kent for the whole of the school summer holidays. My dad and uncles stayed in London to go to work. But they came down to the hop farm at the weekends."

Continued on page 16

A HOP-PICKING SUMMER

When the hops were ready to be harvested, there were not enough local workers to pick them. That's why farms needed extra help.

The whole family helped pick hops!

Hop bin

The stems of hop plants grow up tall poles, clinging to strings.

The hop pickers pulled the stems down to the ground. Then they quickly picked the green hops from the stems.

Each family had their own bin to fill with hops. Then a farm worker, called the tally man, recorded the amount of hops picked so the family could be paid.

Metal hopper hut with curtains added

Hop picker

Peeling potatoes for supper

Boiling water for tea on a fire

The huts were lit by small lamps that burned oil. There was no electricity!

Barry (Born 1943)

"I can still remember how fresh the air smelled in the countryside. When we weren't helping to pick hops, us kids swam in ponds and the nearby river. We also went scrumping, which was stealing apples from the orchards next to the hop farm! At night, everyone sang songs around the camp fires."

A DAY AT THE ZOO

In the late 1800s and early 1900s, a visit to the zoo was very different from today.

Both adults and children could enjoy elephant rides. Children might also ride a camel or giant tortoise, or be pulled in a cart by an ostrich!

Now we know that wild animals feel stress when they are made to do things that are not **natural** for them.

Today when we visit zoos, we try not to disturb the animals. We learn about protecting them and their wild habitats from a distance.

An elephant ride in 1890

Giant tortoise

A chimpanzees' tea party in 1958

Young chimps were trained to take part in tea parties. Sometimes they even wore clothes! Zoo visitors loved to watch the fun. However, today, we understand it is cruel to train wild animals to do shows.

Evelyn (Born 1943)

"In the 1950s, we often visited London Zoo and took food to feed the animals. The elephants would stretch their long trunks towards us over the railings around their enclosure. We would stretch back and feed them currant buns!"

SATURDAY MORNING PICTURES

In the 1940s and 1950s, very few families had televisions.

For a Saturday morning treat, children went to the pictures, or cinema. Hundreds of children packed a theatre – with just two or three adults to take charge.

The entertainment included cartoons and a movie. It ended with an episode from a **serial**, featuring characters such as Tarzan, the Lone Ranger or Batman.

Each episode of the serial ended with a **cliffhanger**. To find out what happened next, kids had to wait until next Saturday!

Children could buy sweets and ice cream to eat during the show.

A queue for Saturday morning pictures

Part of the fun of Saturday morning pictures was being in a club. Kids were given a badge to wear and sang a special club song before the entertainment began.

Kids who went to ABC cinemas belonged to the ABC Minors club.

SATURDAY NIGHT DANCING

In the 1940s and 1950s, Saturday was the night to go to a **dance**.

In every town and village, there was a dance hall. In big cities, night clubs were also a place to go dancing.

All the dancers dressed up, with women in colourful dresses and men in smart suits or their military uniform.

As a band played the latest popular songs, couples filled the dance floor to jive, rumba, foxtrot and tango.

A dance in the 1940s

The jitterbug was a fast, energy-packed dance. Couples would leapfrog their partner, swing each other high into the air and even do the splits!

This couple are jitterbugging at a nightclub in 1951.

Eddie (Born 1933)

"On Saturday night, I'd put Brylcreem on my hair, while mum pressed (ironed) sharp creases into my suit trousers. Then it was off to the Palais Ballroom to go dancing. I met my wife there – 73 years ago. I was 19 and she was 17. I can still remember the beautiful, bright green dress she was wearing!"

GLOSSARY

bathing
Another word for swimming.

century
A period of 100 years.

cliffhanger
An exciting ending to an episode of a serial. A cliffhanger makes the audience want to see the next episode to find out what happens.

dance
An evening or afternoon social event where people pay to go into a hall or club to dance. In the past, young people regularly went to dances on Saturday nights.

historical
From history, or the past.

knitting pattern
A printed set of step-by-step instructions that show all the stitches needed to knit an item such as a piece of clothing.

memory
Something remembered from the past.

natural
Made by nature, not made by humans.

past
A time that has already happened.

respectable
A good, proper or correct way to act.

serial
A story told in episodes or parts on TV, or in the past, at a cinema.

INDEX

B
bathing machines 4, 6–7

C
cinemas 20–21

D
dances 5, 22–23

F
fish and chips 12–13
food and drink 4, 10–11, 12–13, 14, 17, 19, 20

H
holidays 4, 10, 12, 14–15, 16–17
hop picking 14–15, 16–17

S
seaside 6–7, 8–9, 10, 12
steam trains 10–11
swimwear 6–7, 8–9

Z
zoos 18–19

Answers pages 4–5: 1: A bathing machine, see pages 6–7. This is Queen Victoria's bathing machine. **2:** A picnic set, or hamper. Before people could easily buy take-away food in boxes and plastic packets, they usually made their own food for a day out. They might even take a picnic set with plates, cups and cutlery. **3:** A whelk and its shell. A whelk is a type of sea snail. In the past, whelks were a favourite seaside snack – eaten with vinegar and pepper. Some people still like to eat these chewy shellfish today. **4:** A lamp that burned oil, see pages 16–17. **5:** A gramophone or phonograph was a machine for playing music. A disc, or record, was placed on the gramophone's turntable and a needle was placed on the record. The listener turned the crank (handle), to make the turntable spin. The sound came out of the large horn. **6:** The people in this photo are dancing the conga at a dance (see pages 22–23). Dancers formed a long line and on every fourth beat, each dancer kicked out a leg.